# Every Season in Word

## By Julia Royston

BK
ROYSTON
Publishing

BK Royston Publishing
P. O. Box 4321
Jeffersonville, IN 47131
www.bkroystonpublishing.com
Phone: 502-802-5385

© 2023

Design: Elite Covers

ISBN: 978-1-959543-30-5

Printed in the United States of America

# Acknowledgements

I thank my Lord and Savior Jesus Christ for giving me another opportunity to introduce more people to you. I thank you that you have entrusted this gift to me. Lord, let your Spirit move through this book to the people who will read it.

To my husband, Brian K. Royston, the love of my life for loving and cheering me on so much that I can be and do all that God has placed in me. I love you...

To my Mom, who is a great support and to my Dad who is in heaven but, I know is proud of me and always encouraged me to go for it. Thanks to all of my family for their love and support.

A special thank you to Rev. and Mrs. Claude R. Royston for their love and support. Papa thank you for using your fine tooth comb to edit this book again.

I dedicate this book to every person no matter the current season in your life. "All New Season in Word" is sure to help you with whatever you face so that you arrive to your destiny. God Bless You in all that you for the King and His Kingdom.

# Introduction

Ecclesiastes 3:1 "To every thing there is a season, and a time to every purpose under the heaven."

I love all of the seasons in a year for different reasons. I love winter because of the clothes that I can wear to keep out the cold. I love spring because I can shed the clothes and enjoy the warmer weather. I love summer because I love to travel, put my feet in a pool and relax my body and spirit. I love fall because of the change in the colors and football. There are seasons in our lives that correspond the seasons in the environment. In your life, you will experience different seasons in your relationships, career, family and finances. No matter what season your life is in, there is a word for you. The book "Every Season in Word" is an inspirational book of poems to encourage you in each season of life.

I wrote these poems as therapy and healing for me. I trust that they apply the same healing for you.

God Bless You!

## Julia Royston

# Table of Contents

# A Good Thing

Doing a good thing, huh?

Wrong time

Wrong tactic

Wrong totally

Marriage is Good, but?

Wrong man

Wrong motive

Wrong move

Ministry is Great, but?

Right caller

Right competency

Right commitment

People are fun, but?

Right connection

Right cohesion

Right compatibility

God is Perfect, Yes!

Right everything

Right every time

Right eternally

**Prayer:** *Lord, I thank You for this day and continue to guide to the right things, people and places in this life that will give you glory.*

# All I Have is Dirt

All I have is dirt
The dirt after my child hood house burned to the ground
The dirt of the gossip about me
That went all around town

Yep, just dirt left of that old building
Up the road and down the street
Where I put my time, energy and sweat
Trying to earn a decent paycheck

There are just piles of dirt, now
Where construction first started
The money was to be evenly parted
But, equipment lays and workers departed

There are piles of political dirt
Trying to legislate what still hurts
While men and woman sit crying
And wipe clear tears on their shirt

What good is dirt if you can't put it to work?
For the common man
Working as hard as he can
The brave, the free and working broke fill this land

This dirt is no good alone by itself
It needs a motive or a purpose
Not like a canned good
On a cupboard shelf

Dirt needs to be placed in a wide open field
In straight rows, ready for seed
To produce our next meal

Dirt should be the foundation
For a good education
Experiments, the arts and technology
To develop the next Einstein prodigy

What are you going to do with the dirt you've been given?
Pick up the shovel of determination
Fill the barrel of motivation
Water the dirt with tears and sweat of frustration
Plant the seeds and flowers of expectation

Don't stand around waiting for hands from the political nation
Get your own weed eater, forget the haters and fight your own
procrastination

Wade through the fear, doubt and thoughts of hesitation
Help your fellow man live with respect not just another idol sensation
Punish those who prey on the rights of children, poor, elderly and mothers since creation
Look to reap a harvest beyond your wildest imagination

What kind of dirt are you made of?
I'm not trying to get in your business
To speak of
But, you take stock
Of your own dirt and determine what it's worth

Remember what your mama said
When something dropped and you thought it was dead
Pick it up, hurry quick
The five second trick
We can save it, it will work
Remember a little dirt sho' won't hurt

**Prayer:** *Father, you created man out of the dust of the ground and it was a master piece. Help me to work with my hands and create those things that bring you glory, honor and praise. In Jesus' name we pray. Amen.*

# Alone God and I

Alone God and I
Close enough to touch in my heart
Without the naked eye
He's my comfort and guide
A shield and protection
Never really alone
His love will always abide
You love me through it all
Each turn, hill high, valley low
You listened for my every call
I seek you now for direction
Which way, which exit
Which person, place or thing
Don't let me miss my connection
Your perfect will is my plea
Not my will, wants or need
But my blessings are all wrapped up in thee.


*Prayer:* *Father, thank you for keeping your promise that you would never leave me nor forsake me. I long for and enjoy our time together. Amen.*

# Are you a Praiser or a Worshipper?

A Praiser says, I feel like praising him today
A Worshipper says, I worship God no matter what comes my way
A Praiser says, I praise him for what he's done
A Worshipper says, I worship him because he's worthy and the only one
A Praiser says, I praise him for a car or spouse
A Worshipper says, I worship him for he's the creator of man, animal and even mouse
A Praiser says, I thank him for my home
A Worshipper says, I worship him because he sits on the throne
A Praiser says, I sing unto God because I have a great voice
A Worshippers says, I bow down and worship because it's my choice
A Praiser can praise God in a crowd with their face in the place
A Worshipper just needs a closet or bathroom to seek God's will and His Blessed Face

**Prayer:** *Father, help me to worship and praise your name no matter what. Amen.*

# Awake, Awake

Awake, awake
My soul is at stake
Acting phony, sitting, pushing, shoving
Just to be great
It's too late for just a long name plate
Titles in front and initials behind your name just for others to
degrade
Yes,
Souls are dying
Babies crying
Churches lying
'cuz sinners aren't buying
Crossed legs keep on switching
Ears are itching
Muscles are twitching
It's the gospel not you we're pitching
Your message doesn't reach
Come on preachers, stand and preach
Souls to reach
Classes to teach
Hell is real
Heaven we've got to fill
God is waiting to do the appointing
With his holy oil the anointing

To his voice keep listening
Stop halting and resisting
The harvest is ripe, the fruit is falling
Just say yes, the master's calling


**Prayer:** *Lord, help me to continue to say yes to Your will and no to my convenience. Amen.*

# The Birth

The burden of this baby is great

And heavy is the unborn in spite of its weight

The feeding of the inner being

The new life will soon be appearing

Am I prepared?

Is everything ready?

Is the heartbeat still steady?

The heart of the carrier of the seed is racing fast

The time went quickly and it's almost over at last

The midwives are ready to assist

When the time is right

When is the birth date?

Will it be morning, noon or night?

Delivery is sure

So we must endure

Be ready to push, bear down, weep and breathe

This birth is a great one and its Father is the King!


*Prayer:* *Father, I thank you for the purpose and destiny that you have conceived inside of me. Help me to bring to fruition the mission that you have placed on my life.  Amen.*

# The Book

Well, I lost the book
Now before you give me that look
Let me explain
I'll make it simple and very plain

I left it at my mother's
Then I left it at my father's
I left it at his girlfriend's
Or was it one of my friend's

Anyway and anyhow
It's lost
I really don't know how
Now before you have a cow

I left it on the bus
The monitor was rushing us
You know how fast they make us get off
I was sleeping, probably nodding off

I think it fell in the stream
Mrs. Royston, don't look so mean
I'm sorry that it's lost, I think this time for real
Can't you get another one, it's no big deal

Let me tell you, before you start
I was holding the book at my heart
But, I let my brother or my sister read it
While washing dishes and the faucet wanted to see it

It's just a book, but, it's ruined, anyhoo
I've still got the pages oh, you needed the cover on it too
I'll do better next time, I will, it's true
Here's some money to cover the book and fee due

Sure they're pennies but, at least this time I brought you two.


**Prayer:**  *Father I ask that you bless every librarian in every library throughout the world.  In Jesus' name we pray.  Amen.*

# Chores

I see dishes just more dishes

It leaves me wishing for more than dishes

I see laundry just more laundry

I in a quandary for more than just laundry


Have you ever been hungry for more?

The longing for more than the daily chore

It made you want to leave right out of the front door

But you keep coming back for the ones that you adore


Where is the passion, fire and light?

Where is the thrill of waking to another daylight?

It's buried under the drudgery of duty

Not lit by purpose to a pathway of destiny


The necessary must be done

Imagine a house with dishes, laundry and cleaning left undone

It's a sin, crime and shame

The cleaning police must come

But, what about the human house inside?

The interior dreams unrealized

The lawn of ideas unfertilized

The benefits of education un-materialized


The dishes of duty now in the sink

The dust of determination failing and on the brink

The carpet of continuation threatens to rip

The bathroom of boredom like a faucet's annoying drip


Stop the depression, gloom and sadness

Stop the moaning, whining and madness

Look in the mirror you're still here and alive

Start looking at what's right and the light will arise


You may be tired and weary

But, you're still breathing though the way may be dreary

Stop, look at your circumstance, really

Refocus your eyes, I'm calling, just hear me

The dirty dish proved that there was food on the plate

God, Jehovah Jireh provided on time and not late

The dirty laundry proved that there are still clothes are your back

God, the Almighty won't leave you naked or in lack


The dirty house that needs to be clean

Means that you have a house and not just a bridge or shelter on which to lean

That carpet that needs a few passes of a vacuum

Could have been the grass covering your tomb


Praise God for the chores to be done

Praise God for what you have and know that there is more to come

Praise God and let the dishes, laundry and vacuum sing

Praise God for Everything!

# Direction

I thought of you today
As I went along life's way
I even stopped to pray
I hope that makes your day
In your heart, mind and soul
God wants surrender, let destiny unfold
Ask him, trust him with your everything
He loves you, cares for you, wants what is best more than any-
thing
This is the time and the season
Find his direction for your life
The perfect reason
Where does he want you and
What is the plan only you can do
The timing is critical to make your move
You have only God to please
Nothing else to prove
The provision is made, the dream fulfilled
Only say yes, to the master's will.

*Prayer: Lord, guide my feet in the direction that you have for my life.  Let each step be in the path of righteousness for your name's sake.*

# Dishes

I see dishes just more dishes
It leaves me wishing for more than dishes
I see laundry just more laundry
I in a quandary for more than just laundry

Have you ever been hungry for more?
The longing for more than the daily chore
It made you want to leave right out of the front door
But you keep coming back for the ones that you adore

Where is the passion, fire and light?
Where is the thrill of waking to another daylight?
It's buried under the drudgery of duty
Not lit by purpose to a pathway of destiny

The necessary must be done
Imagine a house with dishes, laundry and cleaning left undone
It's a sin, crime and shame
The cleaning police must come

But, what about the human house inside?

The interior dreams unrealized

The lawn of ideas unfertilized

The benefits of education un-materialized


The issues are not the dishes

The dishes represent what your heart wishes

The dream is still down inside

Hurry up, clean the dishes and go make that dream real right before your eyes


The dishes of duty now in the sink

The dust of determination failing and on the brink

The carpet of continuation threatens to rip

The bathroom of boredom like a faucet's annoying drip


Stop the depression, gloom and sadness

Stop the moaning, whining and madness

Look in the mirror you're still here and alive

Start looking at what's right and the right will arise

# Don't Quit

Don't quit, don't even give in to it
Not today, you can give way
The pressure is great but God's power will accommodate
It's down in you
The stuff to see you through
The spirit is still dynamite
Put your dukes up, you still must fight
Fight the fear, oh so near
Fight the stress, such a mess
Fight the doubt, not an out
Fight the past, it didn't last
This season separates men from boys and women from girls
Fake from the real
Your life revealed
Living holy is a big deal
The cover is pulled sin can't rule
Faithfulness will pay off
Keep going don't stop
Be encouraged, you will reach the top

*Prayer:* *Father, I thank you for reminding me not to quit on you since you didn't quit on me on the cross. You have all of the power and I can do all things through you. Amen.*

# Enough

I want to be your enough
Enough of the love you crave
When you're alone in your dark, silent cave
Enough of the hand to hold
When you're walking through this life getting old
Enough of the whisper in the night
When you're wondering will I ever be alright
Enough of the arms to embrace
When you're living the never ending rat race
Enough of the light for your path
When your candle has gone out from the aftermath
Enough of the spirit in your soul
When your paper's still blank and the coffee's cold
Enough of the pep in your step
When your step is inept and you're feeling near death
Enough of the gold in your touch
When your touch's not solid just mush
Oh yeah I want to be your enough
'cuz you don't have enough
That enough you've got is just weak not tough
Lean on me I'll be there when the going is rough
The money is not enough
He won't come through in the clutch
If you were limping, she won't pass you the crutch
I'll love you even if you're not so suchy much

Yes, I'm your enough, the more than enough

I'm enough when you're broke

I'm enough when you're lonely

I'm enough when you're tired

I've got to be your one and only

But I seem to come up empty

When his shoulders are broad and his pockets have   plenty

I seem to fall short lately

When her breasts are big and her butt is rather shapely

I was there when you took your last breath

And will stick with you for the next and the next

Why am I not your enough?

All the money is mine

I never leave you any of the time

I can be reached constantly and never drop the line

I'm the best lover in this lifetime

I leave you breathless time after time

If there is better, you are a lie

I'll prove it the next time

Let me hear you say it out of your mouth.

Lay it on the line

Enough is enough, you're more than enough

Shout Hallelujah, I've got you, you're mine!


**Prayer:** *Father that I thank you that you are now and always will be more than enough for me.  In Jesus' name we pray.  Amen.*

# Fresh Oil

I have poured out fresh oil
It's not because of your work, pain or toil
My grace is upon you
My favor is brand new
I'm your God and you desire to be mine
No more waiting this is the time
The season is here, so have no fear
Write the vision
Strategize the plan
Turn up the heat
Wave the Fan
The fires of passion in a servant burn hot
So move forward for the kingdom
Or get off the pot
I have given you knowledge and information so great
To guide you through doors and gates
Now the anointing is come
Just say yes, for you're the one.
I promise I won't leave you, never alone
I'm right there with you
Omnipresent and always on the throne

Listen to my voice dear child of mine
I'll love you forever
Your father, so divine


**Prayer:** *Father, I thank you for the anointing that only comes from you. Anoint me afresh that I speak, do and accomplish only what you desire in my life Amen.*

# The Gift

A gift to the nation
Not looking for much appreciation
God is the caller and the resource
He has the power to make it through the course
What must I do to follow you?
Present a sacrifice, holy & true
Humble yourself and lift your eyes up to God
Pure minds, clean heart and no more façade
The time is over to play with toys
Grow up to adulthood
No more little girls and little boys
Give me strength, power and anointing
Moving steady despite any disappointing
Keep the gift sharp, shined and sure
With God as your leader
You shall endure

**Prayer:** *Father, I thank you for the gift that you have placed inside of me. Help me to use my gift to build your kingdom, edify your people and bring someone to a great knowledge of you. Amen.*

# Girls of Presentation Academy

Girls, Girls, Girls
Giggling, angry, often complaining
Witty, pretty, ever debating
Young ladies to women
An awesome balance
High school to college
Leaving adolescence
Dreams soar high
Pie in the sky
My boyfriend don't lie
My body won't deny
They think they're ready
Picking up car keys instead of a bear teddy
It's the process gotta' get the prom dress
One semester down
And soon the graduation gown


**Prayer:** *Father, I thank you for allowing me to meet and work with the girls of Presentation Academy. Bless every girl, every teacher and every parent that has entrusted their child to walk through the doors of 4th and Breckinridge Streets. Be with each one until we meet again. Amen.*

# God is Looking for a Wife

God is looking for a wife
To love, honor and cherish
Not something that is temporary
To fade away or perish
What's love got to do with this search?
Everything and more
Open the Bible, it's in there with little research
Love made God wrap himself in sinful flesh
Came to earth, lived, died on a cross
He passed every test
The church, the bride, the chosen happened long ago
Now prepare for the great marriage in heaven
Stand at the throne
The king longs for and waits for the queen
The earth feels it too
And groans with weather previously unseen
Get ready!
Prepare yourself for the wedding in the sky
It's coming soon not just in the sweet by and by
Forever in heaven with God for eternal life
God's waiting on you, his love, bride and wife

**Prayer:** *Father you are the bridegroom and we are the bride. The bride needs to check her dress again to make sure that the spots are gone and the heat has pressed out all of the wrinkles. Amen.*

# God's Choice

This is my remnant, my called and chosen

You'll be fine, if you stay in this position

Sitting bowed, prostrate, it's your decision

On your knees hugging my feet

Come up to my face the journey will be complete

My countenance is a smile

The pursuit was worth it all the while

My nod is yes

My favor is upon you

The gates of heaven are opened

You're my child and I love you

You are my adored


*Prayer: Father, thank you for choosing me in spite of me. My prayer is that you continue to strengthen me so that I may please you. Amen.*

# Harvest Time

The field is white with crops
Blowing gently in the breeze
The green, the dirt, the fruit so ripe
Heavy and waiting if you please
Where are the workers with hands so raw
From sickles, rakes, hoe or saw
The crop is here
The harvest time of year so clear
But, the workers are they close or near?


**Prayer:** *Father, help me to remember that there is a harvest of souls waiting for the news of your saving grace. Lord, make me always sensitive and use me as an instrument to those who need salvation. Amen.*

# He's So Fine...

Hey girls can I please talk about a man this time

You know I think that he's some kind of fine

Oooo that Denzel Washington smile kind of fine

The body of Wesley Snipes in Blade, Terrence Howard light eyes

Richard T Jones' bald head in The Wood kind of fine

You know your typical fantasy man fine

I wish he would call more often with his self so fine

He says he busy and works most of the time

He's so fine it's hard some time to keep him to myself occupied

Believe you me there are a lot of sisters out there with plenty of time

For somebody, anybody who's a straight, heterosexual, no down low, I

pray, kind of fine

I'm afraid half of the time to even be with a brother this fine

Can't take him to church, 'cause sisters don't have their mind half the time On Jesus but, just keep looking at the brother next to me all the time

Passing their numbers in the tithe, prayer and even communion lines
Heaven help us but, I realize that the harvest of sisters is great all the time

But, the bountiful blessings of saved and want to be   married brothers is scarce at the same time
The clubs are out, some reunions too especially that  family of mine
Those hungry, greasy cousins always are looking to steal any-body's man any time
We go to the movies, yes to dinner too, the usual wine and dine
But, does he love only me, that's hard to tell but, we'll see in time
It's been three years, five months and the days are nine
I'm ready for the next step, white dress, tux, I do and the pastor saying here's the husband and the bride
But, he's okay with the relationship as it is at the time
He says it often, what's wrong? There's not a problem, we're fine!
After three years, what are we waiting on, the clock's ticking away the time

No commitment, just dates, events on the calendar of mine

I'm held up, just waiting for the man so fine to make up his mind

But, in my mind, I'm asking myself most of the time, is this man really mine?

Does he even want to be just mine? Yes, look at this face all of time?

If not, say so or just go and don't waste my time.

Am I really ready for him to go out the door or not hear his voice on my line?

That's the question right there, the issues clear and on the line.

Shall I spend more precious time, waiting, wanting and wishing for this man so fine?

Or do I stop fooling myself and pray to God and wait for a man who will love me all of the time, put a ring on my finger and it's not from the five and dime, stand up before God, a preacher and the church and say, I do and that girl is mine...

That man is some kinda fine.

If the man is not so good looking fine, but will spend his last dime to see me looking fine and help me raise the children this time?

If he has no woman on the side, none of the time, will fight any man who seems to give me too much time,

Move over Denzel, that man to me is looking real fine.

If he brings a check home, rubs my back, feet and sometimes my behind,

takes out the garbage, helps with the dishes some of the time and

goes to church with me all of the time....

Lord have mercy that's the kind of man, that's to me, mighty fine and

thank God almighty I'm next in line.

**Prayer:** *Lord, I thank you that you are preparing the right person to be my spouse. I thank you most of all that you are preparing me for my spouse. At times it gets difficult to wait but, give me the courage, wisdom and ability to wait on you. Decisions made without you can delay, destroy and detour destiny. I want your very best for my*
*life and that includes your will, way and the life-long mate you have prepared specifically for me. Amen*

# Henrietta and Jesse's Legacy
## Tribute to Henrietta Marshall Foree and Jesse Lee Foree, Sr.

I stand on the shoulders of Jesse and Henrietta

Tobacco share croppers with just love and a dream

Born a little more than a generation from slavery

Bondage with masters, lynchings and a life of hatred and the mean


Jesse could never read or write his own name

Chicken was how he was known

Driving fast, working hard and keeping you laughing

That was his Henry County fame


He put an X on every paper in the place of his name

X marks the spot for his character, wisdom, endurance

A care free spirit and exceptionally brilliant

Jesse was his name to claim and he was the King of his Domain

Henrietta was Jesse's love of his life

Many babies from much love and she was a prayer filled wife

The story is she could read, write and teach

Given an opportunity even as a woman, any place she could also preach


She died young, 40 to be exact

She was the glue, tape and nails that kept the family in tact

She found favor with not only God but also with Man

She risked her life for her faith, children and every member of her clan


I never met her but I live to tell the story

Because she's here in our eyes, smiles and the voluptuous female bodies that's her glory

Most of us stand no more than 5 foot three

Standing tall, heads high, we're Henrietta and Jesse's Legacy


As I write this, I feel them and can clearly see

Five generations from them have been born and survived to be

Doctors, teachers, lawyers and preachers too

Entrepreneurs, leaders, care and love in whatever we do

Jesse and Henrietta died not knowing most of our names

It doesn't matter how they died, they lived, their legacy we must claim

Their lives spoke volumes in spite of being cut short

Living to the full, over flowing with love, good, bad and work, life is no resort


Who's shoulders do you stand on to live this life full and free

In spite of the trouble, hardships and the continued fight for liberty

Thank you Europe for another month to salute and celebrate Black History

I offer my testimony as a monument and heir to the Henrietta and Jesse Foree Legacy


#Foree4life

# I Love Me

I love me
Yes, the tall skinny me
The knees that stick out
Bony ankles and legs for days me

You know the girl with just bones and no meat
To pinch an inch is a treat
The nerve of her to be skinny and petite
"I can't help it", she says with a squeak
Skinny Minnie that's me

I love the thick me
Yes, the pleasingly plump stout me
The booty that sits out wide
Breasts that are not shy and a round face with a big smile
Me.

You know that girl that all men are eyeing
Watching her behind moving, jiggling and waving
But their mouth says no I didn't see
You know that they are lying
That pretty big girl, yes, me

I love the shy me
Quiet eyes, small smile
Pretty face but nothing much to say
Doesn't mean I'm not thinking
Ears are open, mind is reeling

You know the girl that you ignore
You think she's sleep but, you never hear a snore
Watch out when you least expect
She'll take her chance
The shy girl, she's got next

I love the bold me
Big mouth, loud as can be
Claiming all of the attention
So much to say, a blabb convention

You know that animated girl
More animated than *Pixar* and *Dreamworks* combined
Head, neck, finger and mouth going
All parts intertwined
Wait a second, she'll tell u what's on her mind

Now maybe you're just average
Not too big, not too small
You speak when spoken to
Or sometimes not at all

You say what's necessary
Don't walk with a big stick
You're far from skinny
Some may call u a little thick

Okay you say, on the outside
I'm not a hottie?
But, what's going inside that head is important
More than what's going on the outside of my body
Behind that cleaned washed face
May lie an idea worth a chase
Inside your ears and behind your nose
Where thoughts bloom and creativity grows

Girl Power for those that still play with dolls and on swings
Let them grow up to be powerful and achieve big things

The Tween Queens are in a very important stage
Let them be filled with courage and high self image, that's not
just a phase

Women, lock arms and unite
Sisters continue the fight to stop the denial of our basic rights.

Now stand up, say it loud
I am a woman
I'm me and I'm proud


**Prayer:** *Father, your word tells us to love others as we love ourselves. Help us to love ourselves as you first loved us. Help us to remember always that we are your children because we love one another. In Jesus' name we pray. Amen.*

# I Love You

I've always loved you
Through all of the hurt and pain
Sunshine and the rain
All of your struggles and strain
I loved you

I loved you even when you act a fool
Out there using all of the devil's tools
I'm still crazy in love with you
I brought you before my father
I told Him, this is the one and one day she'll be true
See my hands, my feet and my side that's how much I'm in love
with you

Remember I'm a husband not a player
Some others dropped you at the curb and cast you to the side
But, I said, I'll love her and marry her
And she'll be my bride

So I came down through generations 40 and two
Just to prove my love for you
Mary carried me first and Joseph too
John carried me last into the borrowed tomb
Girl there was no lengths that I wouldn't go for you.
But, you act like you don't want me
I don' t hear from you for days or weeks

You don't call, write or even text me
I know you're busy but, good grief
You could come by my house at least once a week
I just want to hear your voice
You know I love you, you're my choice

So here's just one more plea

For the love I want from you to me

Just meet, love and follow me

Say you'll love me always

Not just tonight but, for the rest of your life

Love Jesus

**Prayer:** *Father we thank you for your never ending love. Words can not    describe how much your love means to me. You love me so I love you in   return and stand ready to obey your word. I love you too. In Jesus' name we pray. Amen.*

# I'm New

New life, new walk

New right to a new talk

Newness in Christ

The payment and the price

A sacrifice made for me

The rugged cross on Mt. Calvary

I'm clean and free

No longer bound indeed

Free to give, free to love

The spirit in me from above

Free to worship free to praise

Living with the father the rest of my days

Purchased by the father

from the enemy, there is no doubt

Planted in the Kingdom of God

Makes me want to shout


**Prayer:** *Father, I ask that you daily help me to walk in the newness of the Christian life and to be pleasing in Your sight.*

# In Your Arms

In Your arms I sleep
In Your arms I'm at peace
There is shelter from the rain
I'm released from hurt and pain
I'm new and it's a brand new day
Fresh thoughts and paths are coming my way
The road to victory was paved
With rocks, hills, deep valleys and some caves
The nights were long with no one close
To say "it'll be fine" and after God I love you most
The days drag on by the weeks and months
Opportunity will come, just wait, don't hunt
I've got you in the palm of my hand
Angels descend and messages are delivered at my command
So don't weep, beg, pout or demand
For at the time appointed, it shall come and the time is at hand.


***Prayer:*** *Father, I thank you for your comfort in my time of anxiety. I thank you that you carry me in your arms when I want to run ahead and find my own way. You hold my hand like a mother with a child crossing the street. Bless me to walk into your will and plan, holding your strong hand. Amen.*

# Just Come

C for come, a call, a connection to closeness

The "O" says, stay open to my ear, options and opportunities

M is for move, motion with momentum not meaningless

But mobility with a motive

E is for expectation, excitement with no excuses

Come to me I want you and have something to say

Come unto me, stay until, don't ever go away

Come back to me, I miss you and love you

Don't leave or stray

The heart says come

The father says come

The spirit says come

Hope anticipates and love gravitates

For you who answer the call eternity awaits

**Prayer:** *Father, I answer the call. Amen.*

# Knowledge

Learning, learning
The wheels of your mind are turning
To know more and go far
This world isn't stagnate
You've got to keep up to be a Jesus magnet
The harvest is ripe
The economy is tight
Distress is at an all time high
Jesus will very soon appear in the sky
Open your heart and mind
Get all you can, don't be left behind
The past is gone
Memories were nice but
The present has a price
Much discipline and sacrifice
Our destiny must be reached
The gospel must be preached
Come on teachers you must teach
Knock on doors, under hedges and highways still seek
'Cuz souls are dying every week


**Prayer:** *Father, you said that if anyone lack wisdom let him ask of you. I am asking you for wisdom in my search for knowledge. Help me to realize that knowledge without understanding is meaningless. Amen.*

# Live Your Life

Sister, Live your Life

Be your best, don't say,

You know I'm just a blank

But I'm the best housewife

Brother, Live your Life

Be the best man you can be

No matter your job,

Whether your collar's blue, brown or white

Children live your life

Do your best, no excuses

In school, A B or C, for the top continue to strive to be

To one and all

Short or tall

Big boned or small

Cocoa brown, very light or no skin tone at all

Be yourself, the belle of the ball

Shop at Target or Neiman Marcus

Drive a jalopy, Benz or ride the bus

Live in a Condo, house or hut

Be your best, despite any of us

Laugh at yourself

Smile at others

Forgive your enemies

Sometimes your sisters and brothers

You're too cute to boot

The men are fine as wine

Life's too short

Heaven's too high

Hell's too hot

For you not to reach the top!


**Prayer:** *Father, I thank you that you looked at me one day and said, Live! Amen.*

# Love May Not Be Enough

What do you do when love is not enough
You cry and scream
Try to act real tough

You hold on real tight
Thinking that the love that you have
Will make it alright

You talk more
You do more
But, the hallway is empty and they are not walking through that
door

You change your look
Maybe your clothes or hair is the hook
That will bring that one rushing back like a flooded water brook

You cut people off
That don't agree with you
The one that warned you, I think they might be using you?

You want this love to be true
Like the kind in the movies
In the end, the sun always shines and the sky is clear and blue

You thought that he or she was the love of your life
That love is sour
Just daily bickering, anger and strife

That once bright shining light
Is now cold and dark
Like a winter midnight
That smile on your face
When they arrived at your place
Is now a frown and your eyes are rolling at an unusually fast
pace

Kisses are now cold
And our hands we no longer hold
Another day if we're lucky because together we won't grow old

The room will so be silent
The laughter will be no more
The sound of their shoes are no longer heard on your floor

What do you when your love's not enough

Cry a little, grieve the loss

But, move on and don't try to recoup the cost


Life's too short

Your loves too sweet

Wait for the one, the courageous and the brave

For your love they are addicted and until death they will crave


**Prayer:** *Father we thank you for your love. At times, we look for love in all of the wrong places and in the unloving faces. The love of others may fade or cease but, your love remains and will increase.*

# Men, Men, Men

Men, men, men
Short ones, tall ones
Black ones, white ones
Latin ones, Asian ones
A good, strong and loving man
A straight sister wants one
Now before you throw a stone
And say I'm straight but, don't really want one
I know you been hurt by one or more than one
But, who says that's the only one
Try again but, be careful and wait 'til the oven's done
You moved too quick
Fell too hard for the trick
Play hard to get
Make him work, long and hard for it
Don't give away all of your secrets
Just for a dinner, dancing and a movie flick
Meet his parents, kin folks, friends and enemies too
Talk to his co-workers, children and a good credit check you've
got to do
There are some good ones still waiting to be caught
But, a gold digger will be left standing on the corner, left, and not
bought

Work on you and make sure you're ready for a relationship new

Heal the wounds, dry the tears and get rid of the baggage

You and your old relationships, for any man, is just too much luggage

Stop being so mean, hateful and brash

Looking at the current man and in your mind seeing another man in a flash

Remember that was then and this is now

Don't ruin your future with the past hanging around

You just never know before it's all through

What started as a friend, may end in I do!


**Prayer:** *Father, I thank you for the men in the world. You have created man as a leader, protector and covering for women and children. Bless our men to be the men of God that you called them to be. Bless those men who have made mistakes and want to change and make a fresh start. Help women everywhere to be the loving, supportive helpmates that you called women to be. Lord, strengthen the men, strengthen the women and help them guide the children so that we will have strong families. Amen.*

# Morning

Morning fresh and clean
The birds come out to sing
The stirring of pots
The off button on alarm clocks
It's morning, a brand new day
Grace is offered, mercy doesn't delay
Faith renewed, love is given, not held at bay
Who loves me this much?
Awakening me with a soft touch
An opportunity to stand upright
Not bowed over with a crutch
God has a plan for this day
Work hard, let him lead you, the path may be gray
But a great reward in this life, he'll pay

*Prayer: Father I thank you for granting me a brand new day. Morning has come and the clock says midnight. I have a new opportunity to say yes to new mercy and grace for this day. Amen.*

# My Way

The struggle
Fighting for position
Strategy always working
With every direction
It's for me, my way no other connection
The anointed seem to be in the spotlight
Shine on me some, I'm alright
Standing in the shadows of a frustrating night
I'm trying with all my might
Struggling, pulling to be seen and heard
I'm waiting in the wings
Understudy? how absurd
I'm a star haven't you heard
Pride in my ability in this struggle is the key
God's not moving fast enough in all his ability
I am smart enough to make it my way,
Don't you see?
Keep going you'll never get anywhere
God sees all and knows every hair
Keep working for yourself
Out of God's will you'll never get there!


*Prayer: I thank you for another day. Help me to not   struggle and work for position but, rest in your decision. Amen.*

# New Level

What do I need to go to the next level?

Family, friends, God and even the devil

Move some things in and other things out

More faith, peace, favor and far less doubt

Add strength, courage and the will to fight

Plus direction from God to make the course left or right

The anointing of God and angelic protection

Morning noon and night

The new level is higher, brighter and further

You've never been this way before

Die to fl esh, flee from sin, love his word and

God's Glory, please fill the temple from the back wall to the door.


*Prayer:* *Father I thank you that You are calling me higher in you. A place deeper in your love, closer to your presence and safe in your arms. Carry me to the level that you have for me and let it be only close to thee. Amen.*

# New Time

The beginning of a new time
The past was bad, good & fine
Time has passed a new day at last
Prosperity destiny & purpose is the forecast
You've waited long enough
The going at times was tough
The hills climbed were rough not smooth
A door has opened now walk through
Look not behind
You'll change your mind
Look straight ahead
Not left or right
God's way is toward the light

**Prayer:** *Father, I thank you for this new time in my life. Help me to continue to walk in Your way and realize that Your way is always best. Amen.*

# Ode to Sheila

Loved to gather there

Where?

The next council did they say where?

The saints gathered each quarter

Dressed so fine and fair

She loved the gathering

Praise the Lord! A smile and wave

Any lengths to get there

Where are we staying, who's church

What's the color that we are to wear

Didn't matter how or who

Just had to get there

In the mix, involved so thick, loved it

Dreamed it, wouldn't miss it!

The only thing stopping me was my body

Separating me from the saints on each and every meeting

Put me in the Lord's presence forevermore

The biggest meeting

Wouldn't miss it, can't believe it

I'm here forever, never to leave again


**Prayer:** *Father, I thank you for the time with my sister. I have joy in knowing that she is safely with you. Amen.*

# One Word

Just one word from You is able to change my life
And make me brand new
Words are power and they are life
One heals, one kills
Another brings pain and strife
The tongue is a member that no man can tame
Full of poison, sharp as a knife
With the heat of a flame
Bridle my tongue Oh Lord
Fill it with grace, hope and truth
Let your spirit dwell in every member
But out of my mouth let only Your words break through
And give glory to you!


*Prayer:* *Father, I thank you that You sent Your word and Your word is able to heal. Your words are spirit and life. Give me only Your words for Your glory we seek. Amen.*

# Path

Stay or go

Yes or no

Stagnate or grow

Left or right

Day instead of night

Have you made a decision or

Still a weak might

Decisions, decisions

Go by faith and pray God's provision

I'm moving but not with a clear vision

The word is so strong

Consuming my thoughts night and day

Looking for black and white

But its hazy and gray

Show me which way

I know my trust in you won't me betray

God's word is there to guide

When the path seems to hide

In God I must abide

For in his perfect will I must reside

Give me a hint

I sadly lament

But, I must wait here patient

Listening closely for the word from heaven sent

Some are chosen, anointed, prepared

Destiny that will apprehend

Others picked a nice, clean path and just went.

When the path seems to hide
In God I must abide
For in his perfect will I must reside
Give me a hint
I sadly lament
But, I must wait here patient
Listening closely for the word from heaven sent
Some are chosen, anointed, prepared
Destiny that will apprehend
Others picked a nice, clean path and just went.


**Prayer:** *Father, the path seems dim and the way unclear but, shine your light on my feet that I may know the path to take. Amen.*

# Peace

The birds don't sing
Not a bell wants to ring
Just the sound of absolute nothing
That's peace

Peace in your spirit
Even breathing, a steady rhythm to it
A child can even hear it
That's peace

A storm is raging
The body's decaying
Your heart's unwavering
That's peace

Your husband left you
His wife left him too
 God said, I'm sticking to you like glue
That's peace

The job went overseas
The boss says the company you must please
It'll work out, just stay on your knees
That's peace

The doctor gave you bad news
They double and triple checked, from every view
You're healed by faith and that's the report you choose
That's peace

Your heart should be racing
The fear suffocating
But, the peace intoxicating
That's peace

**Prayer:** *Father, we thank you for being our Jehovah Shalom, our peace. May your peace rest with us now and always. Amen.*

# Purpose & Destiny

Purpose and destiny
Are coming together perfectly
God's plan for the life he has just for me
The stage is set
The people haven't even met
Or know the reason just yet
Divine appointments
By Consecration and holy ointment
With Dedication to the assignment
Lord, am I ready?
Make my feet as the hind's, rock climbing steady
Have no fear, the end is near
The summit we've just passed
The next level at last


**Prayer:** *Father, you created me and know what you purposed for me to be in this life. Help me to walk in purpose and destiny. Amen.*

# Rely on Me

Rely on Me
I'm your anchor and your source
Lean on me
I'm a strong tower and steady course
Trust in me
I won't tell any secrets
Have faith in me
I won't fail or cause you to regret
Love me completely and freely
I'll love you unconditionally
I won't reject you or cast you away
Come unto me today, don't delay


**Prayer:** *Father I am relying on you for everything in my life. You are my creator and my source. Amen.*

# Rise Up

Rise up and build
The gates lie in waste
Destruction in the Lord's house
Requires much haste
The gates of righteousness are being torn down
The morality standards are lowering to the ground
Where are the keepers of the flame
Who is holding up the blood banner of Jesus' name
Where are the guards, the watchmen on the wall
Those that cry loud, spare not
To sound the alarm and call
Where are the mothers indeed
The wailing women crying out
When there is a great need
Where are the young men and women
Strong and ready to fight
With strength, power, the anointing
And a life
To stand for right
Both day and night
To proclaim the truth
From the basement to the roof

The Kingdom is at stake

Don't sleep now, be ready, alert and awake

God's still coming back

And his children he will take


*Prayer:* *Father, give me fortitude and boldness to stand up for you and proclaim your gospel. Help me to know that the Kingdom of God is worth more than the riches of this world. Amen.*

# Rivers of Living Water

Time of worship

Time of praise

With the fruit of my lips

The name of Jesus we raise

In His presence is the fullness of joy

Not a little but the power full

Don't be shy, standoffish or coy

It's His presence it's not flesh but the spirit that must rule

Invite Him in your heart

And this building

To heal, deliver and His plan revealing

The water is fresh, clean and clear

Get a cup or bring a bucket here

Refresh your body, your spirit renew

Revive your mind

Restore the joy, restart, brand new

Prepare for the battle

It's up to you...

*Prayer: Father, I thank you for the opportunity to be with those who came through the doors of Rivers of Living Water Tabernacle. Have your way in every life and show yourself strong for the struggles that each one must face. Amen.*

# School

You said you loved me
Why did you leave me here?
I am your honey lamb
The one you loved so dear

But, here, why here?
I don't know these people
They are giving me orders
Stand up, Sit down, not there, over here

They tell me when to eat
But the food has no taste
They tell me when to potty
Then they tell me I must haste

Where's my refrigerator
My cup, my spoon my plate
I have my favorite seat at the table
Nobody to tell me eat fast or you'll be late

At the sitters', I used to watch TV, play and take naps
Now I've got a uniform, pencils and a heavy backpack
Not to mention so much to remember
I think I'm having a brain attack.

I want to do it my way
Scribble on the paper, draw outside the lines
They tell me that's what babies do
You tell me I'm your baby all of the time

People telling me stuff
Come in this time, put your stuff here
Don't' do that now,
Then with a smile, we're so glad you're here.

Help deliver me from this awful place
With bossy teachers and healthy food
Take me back to daycare and day camp
I promise I won't scream again or even be rude

I won't survive with these people here
Give me one more rule
What you say I must stay
This is what's called school.

**Prayer:** *Father bless every school system to teach, learn and lead to the next level of abundant living. In Jesus' name. Amen.*

# Spring Cleaning

Dispel forced smiles and phony niceness

Hiding behind hearts cold and lifeless

Laughter that's squeaking and shrilling

Sounds make before a movie killing

Reaching, bending

Groping and rending

Hearts that need mending

Doctor, doctor there are souls that need attending

Emergency, emergency

Dying people all around

Open your eyes and see

The cries of help and please

Where do we start?

Who is first begging to be free?

Start with you, with your heart, get the mop and broom

Clean out the mess of the past

Jesus must have room this is not a tomb

Every closet must be cleared

Pulling the cobwebs as they appear

Get the dust, remove the rust

Retrieve the oil soak the soil

Sweep out the old , Unfold the new

Revive your soul , You'll be amazed at how you grew

New effortless smiles
An ear that really hears
Knowing that in your heart
Jesus lives here!
Teaching you to love not ever hate
Forgive quickly and don't on the other one wait
Give freely of your money and time
God will repay every cent, kind deed and every dime
Keep the mop out don't put it away
The broom to clean up
Any spills or messes
Must go, yes, today!


*Prayer:* Father, I thank you for helping me see the clutter that has gathered in my life. Help me to get the mop, broom and sweep out the unnecessary that I may do your blessed will. Amen.

# Strength for the Journey

Strength, Power and Wisdom
Given freely to those in the Kingdom
Faith, Humility and Trust
These qualities are a must
Envy, Jealousy and Strife
Diminish your anointing
Like soft butter with a hot knife
Grace, Mercy & God's Spirit
Lord fill me up to overflowing with it
In heaven for eternity
In the Presence of God, I'll be
His blessed face to see
The price for sin paid and complete
By the Holy Lamb of God
Perfect, pure and spotless for all humanity


**Prayer:** *Father, I thank you that your joy is my strength. My strength is in you. Amen.*

# The Summit

I don't mind the climb
Every step in rhythm and keep time
Ideas fill my mind
Keep going, working and watching every dime

It just takes one yes they say
I finally said yes that one day
From there it was one, then two and then more
Who knew then, I'd be here with clients galore

After so many years, I've worked every day
Building something the right way
To make my parents proud
To make me proud and say, "I did it!" out loud!

Here I stand on my business and life summit
Not at the top but holding steady so I don't plummet
Standing strong because I worked so long
Night and day, I've earned the word, "belong."

I no longer see the bottom or fear the fall
I'm not at the top and can't quite see how tall
But my feet are firm, my mind is clear
Until I know my next, I'll just sit right here.

# This is the Place

This is the place of my molding and making
The fire, the heat the squeezing and shaping
This is the season of testing and trial
Sometimes approved and welcomed
Other times unashamed denial
The place where everybody knows your success and    failure
The mouth says one thing but thinking you won't endure
When things are good oh, look at the crowd
When things are bad
The place echoes for crying out loud
But through all of the hurt and pain
There's the voice of the master
Saying this is not in vain
The fire is hot but it must be for gold
Purified for my service and my purpose alone
Others I wouldn't try to take to this place
They would embarrass themselves and be a disgrace

But you were chosen, called, anointed for the job
With my power and guide with the elite you will hobnob
Jesus, my son, John, Peter and Paul to name a short few
They suffered for me,
So what about you?


**Prayer:** *Father, I thank you for counting me worthy to suffer for you. Carry me through and help me to arrive as gold to be used by you. Amen*

# Time

Time heals
Time reveals
Time conceals
Time appeals
Time overturns the pain of the past
Time reveals the path that will last
Time brings sunshine in spite of the overcast
Let time do its work just bask
With the healing of time, the wound will mend
Time is what we have, the gift of God to the end
What God has for me, I know it's mine
How I know, the enemy fights me all the time
Time and time again
Inch by inch with much to gain
2003 was a true test for me
Temptations and options, which will it be
2004 so much in store
Experiences, blessings and lessons galore
2005 sometimes I thought I wouldn't survive
2006 was long, hard and the enemy had many tricks
But, 2006 showed me who was the King
And with only God, I conquered everything

2007 completion, fulfillment of the purpose

2007 I must finish what I started before it is gone and soon departed

God the righteous employer will receive a return on his investment royal

God's way or your own way

How can I remain loyal?

Doing things God's way is best

The tests passed bring on the rest

2008,  a new beginning and a fresh start

for all those who waited and believed God in their heart

2009, the God of all space and time

There are great things in store if you are patient and mind

2010, the decade came to an end

If you keep believing and serving, you will win

2011, the view is toward heaven

For power, strength and wisdom from every lesson

2012, and what lies ahead remains to be seen

But, with God all things are possible

His way is still supreme


**Prayer:** *Father, I thank you for each second, minute, hour, day, month and year. Let me live each day to the fullest without regrets. In Jesus' Name we pray.  Amen.*

# True Worshippers

True worshippers are what God is looking for
When you enter God's Holy presence
From the pulpit to the door
You're not worthy, so you bow down
God's the one who gets the crown
You get no honor
You get no praise
Give all to God
Now, today and always
God's the creator of the universe
It's in his hands to bless and curse
Let your worship flow from your lips
Up from your toes, out to your fingertips
Shout it from every mountain and valley low
God is King and Jesus is the most powerful name we know
Enter His presence
Marvel at his existence
Give him all glory; this is the greatest story
How Jesus died the perfect sacrifice for sins
And every believer in Christ wins!
God wants a relationship
Bow down and worship

Change your ways
Give God the praise
Worship is the key to raise windows and open doors
Swinging open to the blessings by the scores
Who cares who taught you how to kneel and bow
Did God get the Glory?
Or did the church just say Wow?


**Prayer:** *Father, you are the maker of everything. We humbly submit ourselves to your will. We worship you as King. We worship you because you are our everything.   In Jesus Name we pray. Amen.*

# Tug Of War

Tug of war it's such a simple game
One we all can name
The pulling, tugging
Falling, calling
Dragging, nagging
Kind of game
You know they're all the same
Tug on the right
You know that feels alright
Then a tug on the left
That's just my old self
They're tearing me half in two
The spirits are warring inside of you
Each limb they want to bend
That wrong thing trying to be my friend
A light pull, so light but, a tug with strength
Says I died for you and shed my blood too
I don't want to tear you down
I have waiting for you a crown
A mansion in the sky
The older saints said "in the sweet by and by"
Let the tug of war game go on
It came only to make you strong

The pulling, to ruling
The tugging to loving
The hustle, to spiritual muscle
The tumbles and great humbles
The fallings to mighty callings
God chose me to rise in victory
One day I'll stand before the King!


**Prayer:** *Father, I thank you that you have all the power over the evil of the world and the evil inside of me. Help me to seek you for help and know that your strength is made perfect in my weakness. In Jesus' Name we pray. Amen*

# Victory

Fight for Peace
War for Joy
Contend for the Faith
Do battle for Contentment

Wrestle the principalities
The enemy is under your foot
Clothed yourself in righteousness
Exchange beauty for ashes

Run from abuse
Flee from misuse
Take flight from the obtuse
Dodge the liars and all of the untruths

Don't answer the critics and naysayers
Don't answer some of what your kinfolks' are saying
Don't answer the skeptics and haters
Don't' answer, just stare like a poker player

Move Forward
Move Onward
Move Pass 'em
Move out of my way or I'll roll right over 'em

Transform my mind
Transform my heart
Transform my spirit
Transform until you transcend

Peace from confusion
Peace from craziness
Peace of mind
Peace from God that always surpasses

Love your God
Love your neighbor
Love yourself
Love your enemy

Sing your own song
Sing when things go wrong
Sing 'til your enemy runs along
Sing 'til I make heaven my home

Victory over yourself
Victory over your problems
Victory over the devil
Victory for eternity

**Prayer:** *We thank you Father because you have already gained the victory for each of us. Amen.*

# Way of Life

Hard work sustained us
when bills were due
Love was the arms that carried us
all the way through
Prayer comforted us
Through all sickness and pain
Like the postman's prayer so go us
Through sun, hail, snow or rain
God will always keep his children on the right course
Destiny and purpose leading every choice
So keep your faith in God
Each and every step you trod
No matter the test
God's way is the best
At the end, head high from your chest
Say it loud, I am truly blessed.


*Prayer:* Lord, help me to keep going in spite of the daily work and obligations of this life. Help me to remember that whatever I do shall prosper. Amen.

# What If

What if you were the second string quarterback
The night of the big game
The first string all-American quarterback injures his   shoulder
Could you come in and throw the ball bolder?

What if you were the understudy?
The night of the play
The actor/actress gets sick and is out
Could you deliver the lines on cue and no doubts?

What if were just a singer in the choir
The night of the concert
The main soloist comes down with laryngitis
Could you sing with the anointing and bring God's      presence to
us?

What if you were the backup musician?
The night of the pre-paid, big gig
The main musician breaks both hands and his fingers won't bend
Could you come in and play the tunes from beginning to end?

What if you were a young preacher in the crowd?
Sunday morning at the first service
The speaker missed his flight and won't arrive at all
Do you have a word in your mouth if you would get the call?

What if you could stop fantasizing and start doing?
Would the dream have been worth the pursuing?
What if today were the day?
Would you be ready for the game to even play?

What if you were given the chance?
Are you ready for the big dance?
What if the way was made?
Would you be ready to make the grade?

What if you were given a dream?
The opportunity comes
The door is open
Are you ready to walk right in?

What if?


*Prayer:* *Father, my life is in your hands. Guide me and help to be ready for all of the "what ifs" in my life. Amen.*

# What's Next?

What's Next for Me?
I'm perplexed don't you see.
With my gift and ability
I must always be moving forward and doing me

I've come along way
Done much and have a lot to say
Tried to do what was right without delay
Even when some didn't want to pay

I kept going and didn't quit
Cried sometimes and often threw a fit
Ate some chocolate, a lot I admit
Throw in the towel, that's not me, that's not it

I'm here I survived
Some may say even thrived
But what's over the hill and around the corner
Where is my next client or the next solid offer?

Assume I'll win, I will definitely not
Walking steady and cautious not quick or a trot
I'm 15 years in this game
After this, I'll never be the same

What's next? Who knows?

In the meantime, down the road, here we go!

Faith walk, no sight

Adventure Begin and screams with delight!

# Who Really Knows You?

Who are the people
Who see you for who you really are
Surely those who are the closest
Not the ones who stand off, so far
You're a King, prince or princess
Who her or him?
There's royalty in our midst
Who called or ordained them?
That announcement I must have missed?
You've known them from a child and brat
But God knew them long before that
He anointed, chose, appointed and destined them
Their life is on a secure map
Your family and friends really love you
Stand with you when you're going through
But when the blessings come
They'll look at them just like news brand new
How did you get this or that, girl?
I said, walking with God.
I thought you knew!

**Prayer:** *Father I thank you for knowing that every good and perfect gift comes directly from you. Amen.*

# Winds of Change

The winds of change are blowing
People are moving back and forth
Coming and Going
Up and Down
They're switching places
The spirit is calling
Changing of spaces
Separating and Intervening
Streamlining and Realigning
Fine Tuning and pruning
Standing and reprimanding
The Holy army is being deployed
Squadrons, companies and battalions
Open your eyes, it can't be ignored
Others are blind and will not see
The invisible force setting up to fight evil from eternity
Watch closely, don't miss it, it's coming in fast
Be prepared, keep working and soon
The great Snatch!

*Prayer: Lord, help me to stand in this time of change. I thank you that you don't change but, times and methods will.  Amen.*

# Woman…

A woman of distinction
Stands apart from all of the rest
A woman of distinction
Still gives it her all, her very best

A woman of compassion
Weeps at the very first tear
A woman of compassion
Works for the cause in spite of the fear

A woman's worth
Is shown by her integrity and no pretense
A woman's worth
Is beyond measure more than dollars and cents

A woman of value
Is recognized by what she does and who she is
A woman of value
Is handled with care, like special occasion dishes

A woman of beauty
Is in the way she carries herself
A woman of beauty
Is not the result of the cosmetic shelf

A woman of honor
Humbles herself and promotes others
A woman of honor
Hands over her last to help any neighbor, sister and brothers

A woman of God
Walks in peace, joy and Love
A woman of God
Will live forever in the heavens above.


**Prayer:** *Father Bless every woman that is on the planet. Help her to fulfill the purpose you have for her life. Guide, protect and strengthen her in everything she puts her hands to do. Give her courage to say yes or no to the things that are not good for her. In Jesus' name we pray. Amen.*

# Working

Working, working

Oh, so busy

A call, you didn't seem to hear

Are you really listening dear?

The noise is so loud

The hustle and bustle of the crowd

His voice is gently and sweetly calling

No fear, just wooing you closer, softly

The comforting hand of the master's touch

The foundation, beginning and never a crutch

I need you every day and every hour

Daily tasks are many but come easy with your power

I must stop

Before I drop

Best in your arms

Is the place from all harm

Working for the King means to me everything


**Prayer:** *Father, I thank you for allowing me to work in your King-dom. Help me to realize that rest is equally as important as work. Amen.*

# More Books by Julia A. Royston

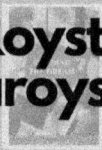

Julia Royston Books
www.juliaroystonstore.com

Julia Royston Books
www.juliaroystonstore.com

# Julia Royston Books
## www.juliaroystonstore.com

# Julia Royston Books
# www.juliaroystonstore.com
# And
# More to Come!